THINKABOUT
Hearing

Text: Henry Pluckrose
Photography: Chris Fairclough

Franklin Watts
London/New York/Sydney/Toronto

© 1985 Franklin Watts Limited
12A Golden Square
London W1

ISBN: 0 86313 280 4

Editor: Ruth Thomson
Design: Edward Kinsey
Additional Photographs: Zefa
J. Allan Cash
Typesetting: Keyspools

Printed in Belgium

About this book

This book is designed for use in the home, playgroup, kindergarten and infant school.

Parents can share the book with young children. Its aim is to bring into focus some of the elements of life and living which are all too often taken for granted. To develop fully, all young children need to have their understanding of the world deepened and the language they use to express their ideas extended. This book, and others in the series, takes the everyday things of the child's world and explores them, harnessing curiosity and wonder in a purposeful way.

For those working with young children each book is designed to be used both as a picture book, which explores ideas and concepts, and as a starting point to talk and exploration. The pictures have been selected because they are of interest in themselves and also because they include elements which will promote enquiry. Talk can lead to displays of items and pictures collected by children and teacher. Pictures and collages can be made by the children themselves.

Everything in our environment is of interest to the growing child. The purpose of these books is to extend and develop that interest.

Henry Pluckrose.

Sit very still indoors.
Try not to move at all.
Listen very carefully.
What sounds can you hear?

Stand in your kitchen.
What sounds can you hear?
The whirr of a mixer,
the hum of a washing machine?

Listen for sounds outside.
Can you hear the distant roar
of traffic,
the rumble of a train?

How much louder sounds would be
if you were nearer!
The express rushes through
a station.
What sound does it make?

The aircraft has just taken off.
The engines roar overhead.

Some sounds are loud.
Others are faint and difficult
to hear.
What is the doctor doing?

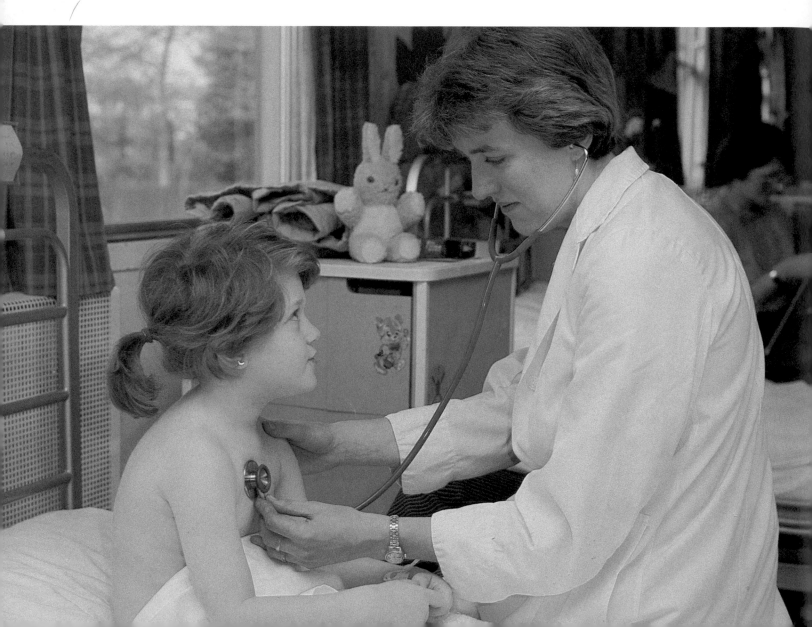

This man is printing newspapers.
Why is he wearing ear muffs?

Some sounds are sharp
and sudden.
A balloon bursts,
then there is silence.

Some sounds seem to go on
for ever, such as the chatter
of people in a busy market.

Some loud sounds give warning
of danger.
What sound does a fire engine make
as it hurtles through the streets?

Have you ever heard
the chiming of bells?
Why are bells rung?

Imagine that you took
these photographs.
What sounds would you
have heard?

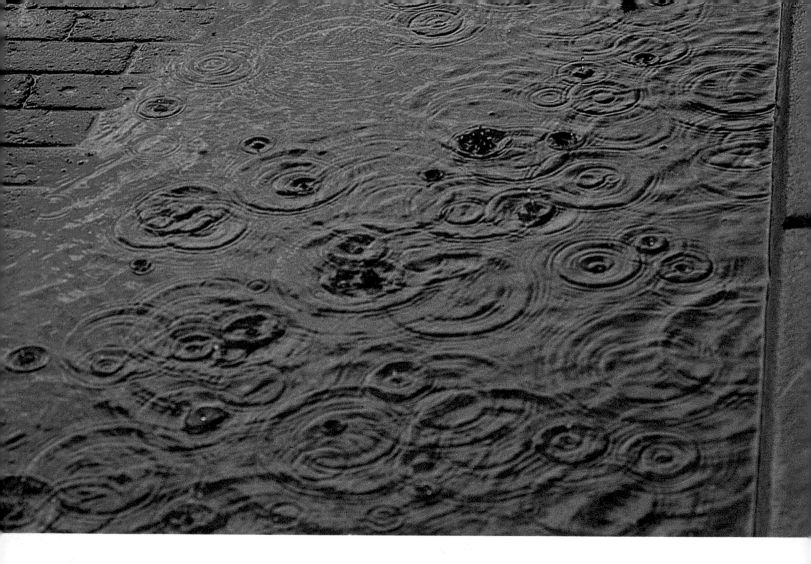

Not all sounds are made
by people or their machines.
Our world is full
of other sounds —
the patter of rain,

the crash of waves on rock,

the crow of a cockerel,

the grunt of pigs,

the buzz of a bee.

Some sounds are gentle
and pleasant,

others are loud
and sometimes frightening,

and some sounds
are so very faint
you never hear them at all.

Sit very still outside.
Try not to move at all.
Listen very carefully.
What sounds can you hear?
What do they tell you?